SCHIRMER'S LIBRARY
OF MUSICAL CLASSICS

SEBASTIAN LEE

Op. 31

Forty Melodic and Progressive Études

For Violoncello

Edited and Fingered by

LEO SCHULZ

Book I contains a Biographical Sketch of the Composer by

RICHARD ALDRICH

IN TWO BOOKS

→ Book I (Nos. 1-22) — Library Vol. 639
Book II (Nos. 23-40) — Library Vol. 640

G. SCHIRMER, Inc.

DISTRIBUTED BY

7777 W. BLUEMOUND RD. P.O. BOX 13819 MILWAUKEE, WI 53213

SEBASTIAN LEE

SEBASTIAN LEE was the eldest and most brilliant and distinguished of three musical brothers, natives of Hamburg, though bearers of an English name. Like his brother Louis, he devoted himself to the 'cello, and became one of the most prominent of the solo performers upon that instrument, known alike in Germany and France. He was born at Hamburg in 1805, and studied with J. N. Prell, who was himself a pupil of the great Bernhard Romberg. His first appearances as a solo cellist were made in 1830, in concerts that he gave at Hamburg and Leipzig. Then he set out upon a tour, visiting Cassel and Frankfort, and arriving in Paris in 1832. There he achieved a brilliant success at his concerts in the Théâtre Italien. In 1836 he gave several concerts in Paris with Gusikow, that singular genius, who excited the musical world of the 30's so greatly by his performances upon the "Strohfiedel,"—an instrument something akin to what is now known as the Xylophone, composed of strips of fir wood resting on a framework of straw. It seems to-day like a curious episode in the career of a dignified virtuoso of the position to which Lee aspired; but it is only necessary to read the contemporary comments upon Gusikow's performances to appreciate the situation. The fastidious Mendelssohn wrote enthusiastically of him as "a true genius," a "real phenomenon, who is inferior to no player on earth in style and execution;" Fétis, the musical Brahmin, called him "a prodigious talent," and wrote with equal enthusiasm of the admirable instinct that taught him the means of producing from his strange instrument the accents of expression and passion. Lamartine and Michaud' were among his patrons, and he was much encouraged by the violinist Lipinski.

Lee then betook himself to London; but soon returned to Paris, wnere he made his home for the next thirty years, being till 1868 solo violoncellist at the Grand Opéra. Retiring in that year, he returned to his native Hamburg, where he spent the remainder of his days. He died there on January 4, 1887.

Like most other virtuosos, Lee published many pieces designed to exploit a virtuoso's powers upon his instrument—variations, fantasies upon operatic themes, divertissements, etc. More important are his numerous compositions intended for purposes of instruction, many of which were primarily written for the use of the Conservatoire at Paris, including a number of duos for two violoncellos entitled "École du Violoncelliste." His "Method" for the 'cello is one of the most widely used of all such instruction books.

RICHARD ALDRICH.

Forty
Melodic and Progressive Études.

SEBASTIAN LEE. Op.31, Book 1.

Down-bow.
Up-bow.

1. Exercise in the broad style of bowing.

Andante.

2. Exercise on the Legato.

Allegro moderato.

3

3. Melodic Exercise.

4. Scherzo.

Allegretto con moto.

5. Exercise on the Legato.

Allegro con moto.

6. Melodic Exercise.

Allegro.

7. Exercise on the Legato.

Moderato.

espressivo

D-str.

Allegro non troppo.   8. Exercise for the Right Wrist.

Moderato.

9. Melodic Exercise.

Allegretto.

10. Rondo.

11. Melodic Exercise.

Allegretto con moto.

12. Exercise for the Right Wrist.

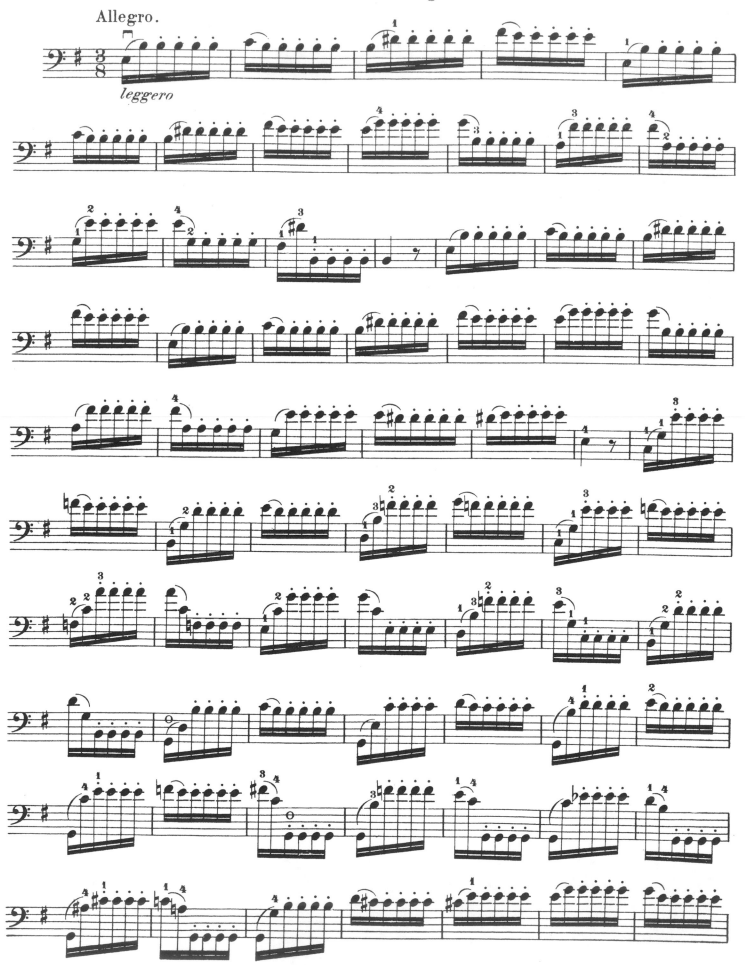

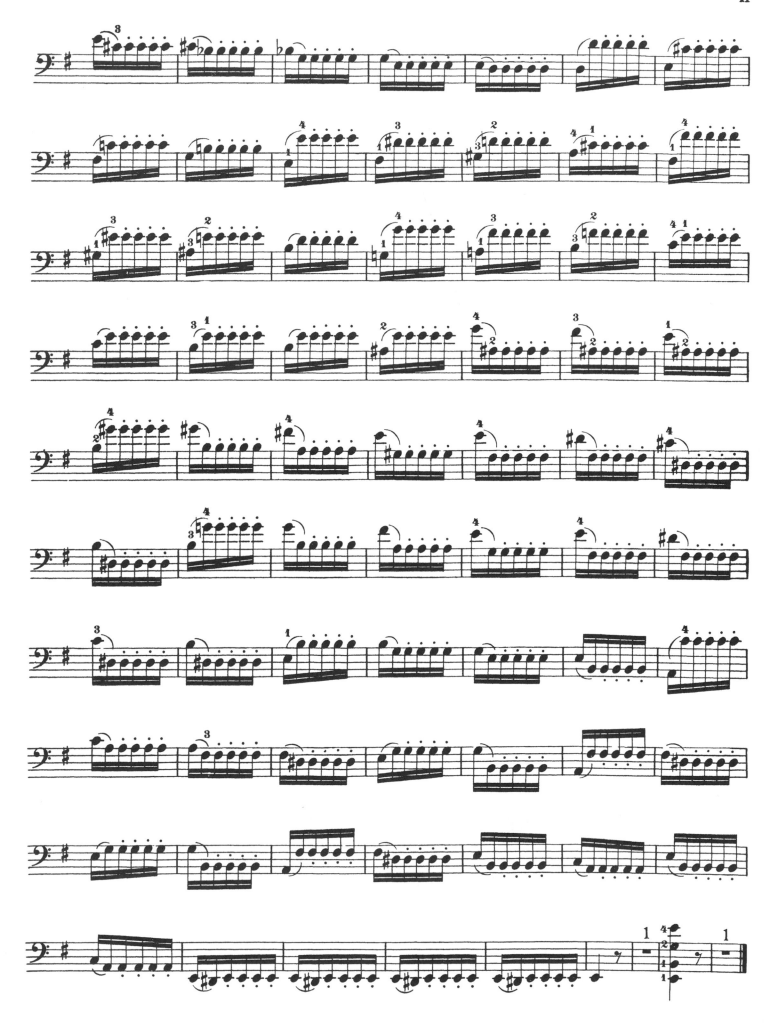

13. Theme and Variations.

13

14. Exercise in Dotted Notes.

Maestoso.

*) Different bowings:

15. Facility in Bowing.

16. Exercise on the Inverted Mordent.

Andante con moto.

Allegro moderato. 17. Facility in Bowing.

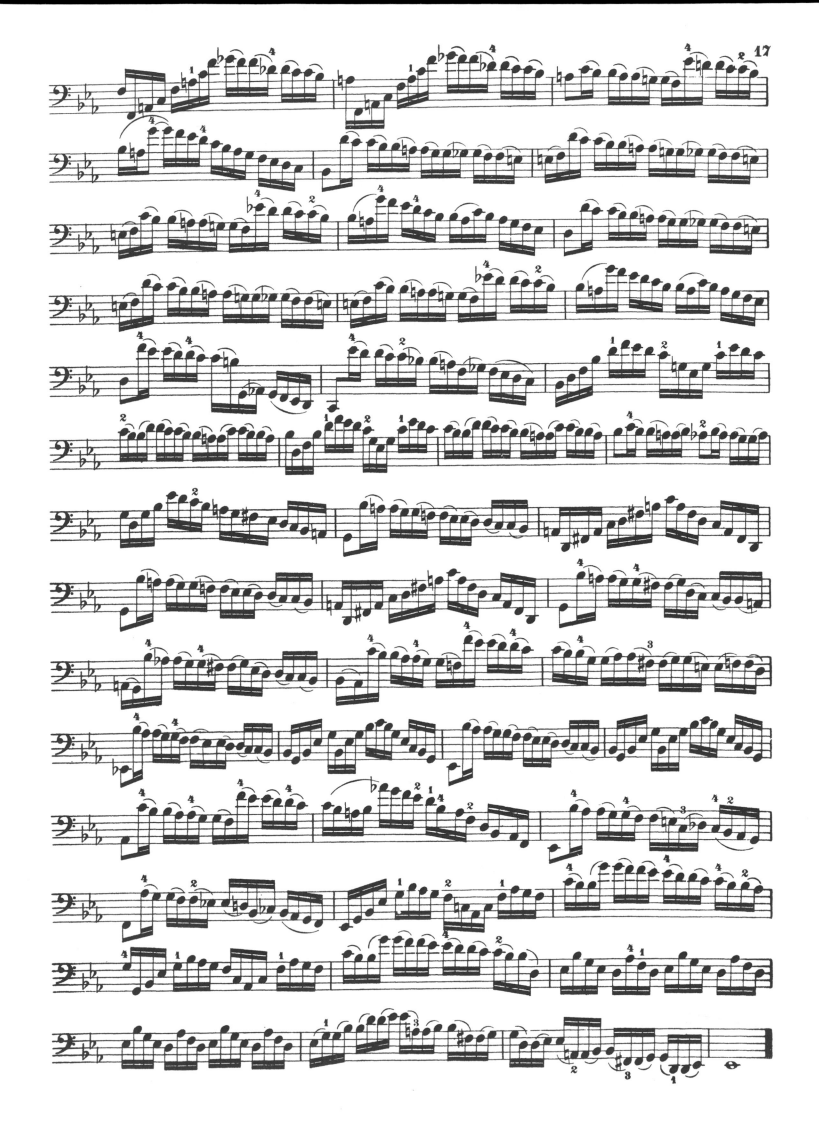

18. Exercise in Detached Bowing.

Moderato. 19. Rondino.

20. Exercise on the Trill.

Allegretto.

G-str.

21. Exercise in employing the Thumb.

Allegro.

same pos.

22. Exercise in Arpeggios.